Djing

A Guide for Kickstarting Your Dj Career Like a Pro and Performing and Spinning Your Way to the Top

By Mike Nash

circumstances is the author responsible for any losses, direct or indirect, which are incurred as a result of the use of information contained within this document, including, but not limited to, —errors, omissions, or inaccuracies.

Contents

Thank you for buying this book and I hope that you will find it useful. If you will want to share your thoughts on this book, you can do so by leaving a review on the Amazon page, it helps me out a lot.

Introduction: What Is A DJ?

When you consider a DJ, you might consider somebody who plays tunes on a radio, somebody who plays tunes at a wedding event or somebody who spins records on decks at nightclubs. DJ is an acronym for a disc jockey, a term that started in the 1950s when radio personalities initially entered the picture. Even though music was played over the airwaves for years prior, the DJ was a character figure who enticed teens. The 1950s was the very first decade where the worth of marketing to teens emerged. As a result, those who played pop music on the radio not just needed to play the leading tracks, they needed to likewise have personalities that the teenagers appreciated to ensure that they would listen in to their broadcast.

The DJ has actually been an establishment in the radio market over the past 50 years, although the function has actually altered considerably, particularly over the past twenty years. In the 1980s, brand-new technology made it possible for individuals to end up being a DJ for a wedding event along with other occasions. Employing a DJ to play music at a wedding event over amplifiers was substantially less expensive than employing a live band. As a result, there was an entire brand-new opportunity opened for those who had substantial understanding of music and the cash to buy the tools.

Home music was likewise born in the 1980s. This included mixing numerous different kinds of music, normally from recordings, and making them into a special noise of their own. This can be performed in a range of various methods, although an excellent DJ who plays in a club is going to utilize vinyl records to produce their own audio. Vinyl records and turntables, once looked at as an artifact of the past after the arrival of the CD and CD players, made a comeback in nightclubs.

Putting it simply, a DJ is somebody with a significant understanding of music, a big collection of music and an understanding of how to play the music in a manner that others will wish to listen to the music. Somebody could be a DJ on the radio, a DJ in a club or a DJ playing for wedding events and celebrations. Even though you must go to school for broadcasting in case you wish to get on the radio, you do not need to have any kind of degree to begin your own enterprise as a DJ who plays at wedding events and other occasions. You do require a following in order to end up being a DJ for a prominent club.

The most essential characteristic a DJ has is a large understanding of music and what individuals wish to hear. The 2nd essential characteristic of a DJ is their personality. Both of these elements integrated can make somebody into a popular and well-compensated DJ. These characteristics are not found out in a class, yet they can be obtained through studying music along with the art of amusing others.

By checking out this book, you will find out how you can begin in the amazing world of spinning records for others. Whether you intend to get a job in a hot club as a DJ, or if you simply wish to do your own thing and have a company where you generate income on the side for playing at wedding events and other occasions, you can accomplish it by following the guidelines that are laid out in this book.

Chapter 1: Discover Everything About Music

The most essential characteristic a DJ needs to have is a large understanding of music. Not simply popular music, due to the fact that this comes and goes throughout the years, but all music. An excellent DJ will understand the appropriate tune to play and when. Even a DJ who mixes vinyl in a venue understands which sounds match one another. Being musically inclined is essential to somebody who wishes to be a DJ. This does not always suggest that they understand how to play a musical instrument, yet they need to understand everything about music, from classical to hip hop, so as to be an effective DJ.

The most effective of all of those in the DJ industry have an excellent admiration for music. They are aware of all the categories and even though they might choose one over another, they recognize that all music is essentially a mix of numerous various kinds of music. Artists today all got their motivation from artists from the past who also got their motivation from artists of the past. Etc.

Think about, for instance, the band Oasis. Not hard to recognize their standard influence, which was The Beatles. The Beatles, meanwhile, were influenced by a range of various artists, consisting of Elvis Presley. Presley was influenced by other artists along with other categories, consisting of the gospel. All music today originates from a range of various categories.

The majority of people believe that the club DJ just spins vinyl utilizing club mixes. Nevertheless, they need to get the music for these mixes in some method. A number of them will utilize a mix of pumped in noise through synthesizers along with vinyl records that they spin in a specific manner in which the sound is modified. By doing this, they are developing a particular sound. This resembles playing a musical instrument. Nevertheless, as anybody who has actually ever tried to play a musical instrument understands, not all the noises that originate from the instrument are excellent. A few of them are destined to be genuine clinkers in case the individual who is playing the instrument does not practice and does not have an ear for music.

Some individuals are created with a natural 'ear for music.' They can pick up tunes in their head and after that play them anew on numerous instruments. They can even make up music in their heads. Sometimes, these artists are taught in order to acquire this understanding of music. In other instances, there is no training included. Sir Paul McCartney, who is probably the most effective author of the 20th Century, has no official musical instruction and can not even compose or read music.

You do not need to be naturally talented in order to acquire success as a DJ, however you do need to understand music. You need to have an ear for which sounds work properly with others, particularly if you are thinking about a livelihood in this field. Even if you are simply searching for a job as a DJ who hosts wedding events and celebrations, you want to understand the appropriate tunes to play in addition to when to play them. The DJ at any wedding event is generally like the emcee of the wedding event. They get the ball moving when it concerns dancing, getting the audience on their feet, settling them down and after that getting them to leave when the night is finished.

If you wish to be a radio DJ, however, you will have a directory of music at hand. You still want to understand the appropriate tunes to play, nevertheless, the majority of those who work in radio work for a particular station that plays a particular category of music. When it comes to being a radio DJ, personality is the essential characteristic. Odds are your audience have actually heard the tunes you are playing over and over again, and can quickly acquire them. Those who tune into your program will wish to hear you, along with any information that you can supply to them about the kind of music that they are tuning in to.

The very best method to get an ear for music is to analyze music and listen to it. Discover what kind of music mixes well with another kind of music and practice producing your own noise. The most effective club DJ s in the market have their own special audio that brings individuals in to listen to them.

The more you listen to music, the more you are going to discover. You need to embark on this research study just as you would any other course. Along with discovering the titles of the tunes along with everything about the category, you need to find out about the artists and the musicians who made these tunes popular. You ought to likewise find out a bit about music history in order to succeed in this field. Once again, the more you continue to listen to music and have an admiration for the music, the greater you will be at ending up being a DJ.

In addition, you want to have a big collection of music available. In case you are intending on spinning music at a club, you want vinyl albums in addition to recorded music. You might download music from the web so as to get this to play as you turn the vinyl. The majority of those who start in the industry begin with the minimal quantity of devices.

Whenever you listen to music, odds are that one category will interest you more than any other kind of music. You need to choose this category if you are going to succeed. Those who are the very best in this industry are those who have genuine passion for the music that they play. The audience can feel if you have a passion for the music and will react consequently. If you are simply playing music to satisfy the crowd, yet not yourself, odds are it will be obvious and you will not achieve success. Even worse than that, you will begin to dislike your task. You ought to enjoy the music that you play as though you are producing it yourself, as an art form, so as to end up being a really effective DJ in any kind of market.

Preferably, take a music class. Discover how to play a musical instrument. You can likewise take a history of music class for more information about the various categories of music that are available and how they originated. The more you find out about music, the much better you are going to be at ending up being a DJ.

Chapter 2 - Getting The Right Tools

Before you can wish to end up being a DJ, you want to purchase the ideal devices. You are going to wish to make certain that your audio is well heard. You can buy devices that cost thousands of dollars, or begin with a turntable and some downloaded music that you place on your computer system. You ought to likewise have an amplifier that will have the ability to crank up the volume.

One crucial thing to keep in mind about music devices is that you get what you spend for. If you wish to end up being effective as a DJ, you are going to want to continue to purchase better tools so that you can enhance the quality of your audio. The better the amplifier, the better the audio. You want to have a really clear audio in order to get the folks dancing.

Computer systems have actually made it simpler not just to obtain music yet likewise to play it to others. Nevertheless, the stereo noise that emits from the majority of computer systems is unsatisfactory to play for others in a venue. You must buy tools that will allow you to begin so that the audio that you play is not just audible, yet clear too.

A microphone is likewise necessary if you are going to be a DJ. You are going to be more than merely a record spinner, you are going to be a character. This implies that you need to speak over the mic whenever you are playing your music. A few of those in the market will utilize the mic in an imaginative method to additionally magnify the audio. You can get a novice set if you wish to be a DJ for about one thousand dollars. This will offer you all of the devices that you require to set up in a club and have the ability to spin vinyl in addition to mix in your own music.

There are different methods to get the devices that you require to end up being a DJ. The very best method to purchase these devices is to get it used. You can typically get a much better offer on secondhand devices than you can on brand-new devices and likewise get better quality for your cash. Purchasing devices from a DJ who is either failing or one who is updating their devices is the most ideal method to get a deal on what you want for your outfit.

A turntable is the most important tool for the club DJ. This will allow you to play vinyl along with mixing your own music to the noise of the vinyl record. You can navigate the vinyl record in a manner that you can not do with a CD to provide even more distinct audio.

You want to have a method to be in a position to have the sound heard. You likewise can utilize a synthesizer as a method to misshape the noise of the music, once more to produce your own music. This can produce an electronic quality to the noise that you are playing. This might or might not work effectively with the audio that you are attempting to develop.

In other words, you want to have a method to play music to individuals so that they can hear it effectively, over a series of speakers and amplifiers that are linked to the speakers. You must have a volume control board so that you can have fun with the noise. If you are intending on spinning records, you want a turntable so that you can likewise produce your own distinct music. Additionally, getting a synthesizer is an excellent strategy to make your audio special. A microphone is needed to have your voice heard.

A few of those who begin in the DJ industry start with few devices and slowly start to build themselves up. Think about older rock bands, for one minute. They did not start with the most effective instruments when they initially started playing. In case you have a great audio, and it is clear and loud enough for individuals to hear, you can then begin to contribute to your tools as you move along.

Obviously, the most crucial tool that you can have as a DJ is a big directory of music. You can get music from numerous sources, including online downloads. You need to have your music arranged in such a way that you understand where everything is which you can play the appropriate music at the correct time. The more music you have, the more effective you will be when it comes to being a DJ.

When you are searching for vinyl, you can search for used records along with brand-new. New vinyl albums, which used to be once the gold standard when it pertained to what individuals used to listen to, have actually soared in price in the last few years. Since the CD ended up being the gold standard of music listening in the 1990s, vinyl albums went by the wayside. There was a revival in vinyl in the early portion of the 21st century and now numerous artists are recognized when their music comes out "in vinyl." A vinyl record is a 33 rpm record that plays on a turntable with the utilization of a needle. Once, this was among the handful of ways that individuals had the ability to listen to music that they acquired.

Today, obviously, there are numerous possibilities to get music. You can download a mix of music straight off your computer system and put it to CD. You can likewise acquire CD music from a range of various sources. If you are intending on being a club DJ, you may wish to try out various kinds of categories when it concerns your music, so it pays to have music from all various kinds of categories. If you are intending on getting gigs as a wedding event DJ, you need to likewise have a big selection of music, specifically popular tunes and dance music. You wish to have the old standards in addition to the most recent hits when you are intending on hosting celebrations or wedding events so that you can accept requests.

There is no reason for any DJ to be without music these days. Since it is so simple to download from the web, and practically any tune is accessible, you can develop quite a collection of music when you are coming to be a DJ. Getting the music is not as crucial as arranging it in such a manner that you understand precisely how to get to it and when. You can do this by means of your computer system. The majority of the DJ s today will utilize their computer system and laptops as a method to arrange their music so that they can get to a particular song within a matter of moments. Having your music arranged by computer resembles how music is arranged in a radio station. The more arranged you are when it concerns your music, the greater you will be at being a DJ.

When you have the appropriate devices for your endeavor as a DJ, huge understanding of music along with the music itself, then you are ready to start your work as a DJ. Like any other kind of music that you discover, you need to practice before you essentially go out there before the audience. The more you practice, the greater you will be. Think about the concept of using up the violin and after that playing in an orchestra the initial time you ever dealt with the instrument. You should not try to be a DJ without considerable practice.

Chapter 3: Try Out the Music

Practicing being a DJ is like understanding to play a musical instrument. Both of them take a skilled ear for what appears excellent and what does not seem excellent. Both take practice and time experimenting with audio. You can begin to explore various sounds as soon as you have all of your devices prepared.

You must have a space where you can practice where you are going to not just not disrupt others, yet likewise where you will have the ability to hear quality audio. You need to mute out as much other noises from the location as you can so that you can produce somewhat of a soundstage. This will offer you a much greater concept of what you are playing and the audio itself.

Begin by experimenting with various kinds of music from different categories. You can utilize mixing devices to get various noises that might or might not work. If you are intending on ending up being an effective club DJ, bear in mind that the secret to the music is to get individuals to dance. Actually, the secret to any DJ music, with the exception of the radio DJ, is dancing. So you are going to wish to ensure that you have a great backbeat to the music that can produce the dance music.

You must have some kind of taping tool that you can utilize so that you can really hear the music that you are playing. You need to record all of the music that you play due to the fact that you never ever know what will work. You may like a specific part of what you record, yet dislike another part of the exact same music. By tracking the music that you are playing, you are going to be better able to develop mixes.

The more that you explore music, and also with the turntable to make it more powerful dance music, the greater your music will end up being. When you are positive that you are producing a noise that is not just pleasing, has an excellent dance beat and is something that you can quickly recreate, you can then begin by enabling buddies to come over to take a listen. Producing music as a DJ is an art form. As holds true with any other kind of art form, the majority of people are comfortable sharing their art after they believe that they are a bit more self-assured in what they are doing.

Initially, you might feel as though you are simply producing noise. As you start to get more knowledgeable about the noises that you are developing, nevertheless, the more the sound will become something more enjoyable and something that others will wish to hear.

Among the most crucial elements about being an effective DJ is developing your own sense of sound. This holds forth for any kind of artist. A DJ needs to consider themselves an artist of sorts. The most effective of all artists are not those who just copy what others are playing, yet put their own special spin to the sound. Be bold and begin to get as innovative as you wish to be when it pertains to playing your music.

After you have buddies over to listen to what you are spinning, take their suggestions, but with a grain of salt. In case you feel strongly about a piece that you developed, do not feel dissuaded even if somebody else does not like it. There is a whole list of artists who were rejected by those who were prominent in the market due to the fact that they did not match the model of what was marketable. The real musical artist plays what they feel in their soul, not simply what others wish to hear.

That being stated, if you wish to get gigs, you are going to need to provide individuals what they desire. George Harrison may have had the ability to get individuals to sit through hours of Sitar music at the "Performance for Bangladesh," yet until you have actually gotten to his status, it pays to play something that is marketable yet has a tad of an edge to make you stand apart a tad more.

By sticking out amongst the others, you will not just produce your own audio, but likewise establish your own following. Having your own following is an important part of being an effective club DJ. As it holds true with the wedding event DJ, who gets the majority of his gigs by word of mouth, the exact same holds forth for the club DJ. The more individuals who come to listen to your specific audio, the more prominent you are going to be. As soon as you get to this point, you will have the ability to compose your own ticket when it pertains to spinning music in venues.

Do not hesitate to try out various kinds of music. Take music from all categories and blend them together to develop your own unique audio. Keep in mind that all music is usually related in some way. The more you try out the various kinds of music, the greater it will be when it comes to establishing your own special music. You can hit on something that is going to have folks demanding to listen to what you spin.

Likewise, consider other kinds of music, besides simply popular music. A number of those in the DJ market today are checking out ethnic music as a means to develop a distinct audio. You can put in African, Arabic, Asian or other kinds of music into your mix. Your mix that you produce does not need to include all American or British noises. Utilize folk music and music that is conventional to other cultures if you wish to truly develop something different.

The more you continue to explore music, the greater you will end up being at being a DJ and you will begin to develop more music. Do not be shocked in case you get hooked on a particular music when you start and after that follow it until you discover another music that you like better. Artists are not meant to be stationary, and a spin DJ is an artist. You might not play a musical instrument within a band, yet you are amusing individuals as though you were doing just that. You are composing music by blending in a range of various music together so that you mix your own distinct music.

Chapter 4: Learning To Become An Entertainer

Along with being well knowledgeable in music and having a large understanding of sound, a DJ likewise needs to be an entertainer. You can most likely select some rock stars in your head who you have actually seen in concert. A few of them are born entertainers who thrill the crowd. Others are not comfy performing in front of others and prefer to be recording and creating music. A lot of effective artists today need to have some kind of magnetic performing magic to them so as to get heard. Even older groups that have actually been around for a number of years are still touring to advertise their music and get their enthusiasts jumping.

In addition for your passion for music, you likewise need to have a passion for people. When you are playing music for folks, whether you are at a nightclub or at an occasion, you need to like the people. This is not a profession for a diminishing violet. It is a profession for somebody who is sociable and who genuinely delights in entertaining the audience.

The component of being a DJ is being a character. Somebody who is an artist with the music yet who likewise understands how to get folks in the state of mind to have a good time. Once again, the DJ is the emcee of any occasion, so you mustn't hesitate to get your voice out there.

How do you get to the point where you are prepared to have your voice heard and do not feel reluctant about speaking in front of folks? You practice. The very first biggest worry of the majority of people is speaking in front of an audience. Second is death. Yes, death is second to speaking in front of an audience. Nevertheless, when you can get used to speaking in front of folks and captivating them, it is simple. The first time you perform as a DJ, you might feel a little worried. However as you continue with this profession, it is going to get simpler and simpler for you.

Years back, a radio DJ was the only DJ available. They all had gimmicks. As competitors grew, so did the requirement for an audience. So they began to come up with different ways that they might get listeners to their stations. Among the most prominent of all of the big-time radio DJ characters was Wolfman Jack. Individuals listened in to his broadcast not so much to hear his tunes that he played, yet additionally to hear him. Along with playing music, he would receive calls from listeners. He was a legend in the market up until his passing. He had a really gruff voice and would typically howl, like a wolfman, hence providing him the name. Throughout the years, individuals have actually attempted to come near having this kind of following, however nobody quite did.

These days, radio personalities are typically talk show personalities. Few who play music have a cult-like following such as Wolfman Jack. However in case you wish to be a DJ in a club and even play at occasions, then you want to establish a character that is both your own, along with fascinating to others.

Although the gimmick may have worked wonders years earlier, a gimmick today appears corny. Unless, naturally, it does not appear like a gimmick. Wearing a particular kind of clothes can make you stand apart. Having a specific accent can make you stand apart. Talking in a specific way might make you stand apart. Obviously, your music is the most vital part of your DJ profession due to the fact that without that, no gimmick on the planet will continue to hold you up, yet if you can integrate an outgoing character that has a special quality to it along with fantastic music, you could truly have it made in the DJ realm.

The most fundamental part of establishing your DJ character is to establish your own personality. Not the personality of another person. You are going to wish to be yourself, yet likewise take advantage of what sets you apart from other folks. There is something that sets everybody apart from everybody else. No two individuals are clearly alike. Utilize the thing that is unique about you, that makes you distinct, and take advantage of it in order to provide yourself your DJ personality.

A fake personality is generally seen right through by individuals. You do not need to be outrageous, either, if you wish to be an effective DJ. Think about all of the outrageous stars who are out there today - do we actually need another one? Maybe you can develop a personality that is a tad downplayed instead of overemphasized yet still makes you stick out so as to get your music heard.

Enter into any venue where there is a DJ and take a look. Instead of simply taking a look at individuals in the club or the music, take a look at the habits of the DJ. See what about them makes the audience like them. For the most part, you are going to see that they all practically act in the same way. They all have their list of tunes that they play, all utilize the very same expressions, the identical slang and are all quite alike.

Success is attained by uniqueness. Consider what you might do in a different way that would make the crowd not just stand and notice your music, but likewise you. Take a look at how the various DJs in the club dress. The kind of accessories and hats that they use. Can you imagine anything that would make you stand apart that you might do in a different way?

Sure, you can constantly get to be more extravagant. However this is simply another gimmick and will just last up until another person gets even more extravagant than you. Possibly you might do something that is distinct, that is all your own, and get others to watch. Possibly a various style of clothes. A various method of mannerisms. A various method of speaking that is going to make you stick out above the others. Standing apart above the others is nitty-gritty when you wish to succeed in any kind of show business, and make no mistake about it, being a DJ belongs to show business. Whenever you captivate others, you belong to show business.

One manner in which you can deal with your personality is to experiment with your buddies. As soon as you get used to performing your spinning in front of individuals who you understand, you are going to feel more comfy with individuals who you do not know. A few of those who enter into the DJ industry wind up bringing somebody with them to help them out.

Previously, we discussed being a DJ at a wedding event or other kind of gathering. The majority of the time, a DJ will need to begin generating income by doing this. You might not have the ability to spin the kind of music that you are wanting to play, nevertheless this is an exceptional method to generate income along with getting used to entertaining individuals. It likewise can help you establish your DJ personality.

It is essential that you have an outbound personality when you are a DJ and that you like to get along with other individuals. You must like to captivate. However do not permit your personality to take control of your music. Bear in mind that music is the primary reason that individuals are visiting clubs or dancing at wedding events. They are not there to see you, you are part of the fun yet not the fun itself.

The more you exercise your personality abilities in front of others, the greater you will end up being at this industry. The more gigs you get, the more your self-confidence will increase. Sure, there are going to be times when you are off your mark a tad, however this occurs to the very best of entertainers. Do not let it get you down. And never ever let any sort of frustration, such as a rejection for a job, hinder you from what you wish to do. The most effective individuals in the show business have actually dealt with rejection consistently. Constantly bear in mind that "Rolling Stone" stated that "Led Zeppelin" would never ever cut a decent record.

It might take you a bit before you end up being comfy with your DJ personality. It might alter over a time period. This is alright. Once again, entertainers are constantly altering with the times. Even more essential is the fact that you need to keep your finger on the rhythm of what is prominent with the audience when it pertains to music. This is constantly altering too. A great DJ has a shimmering personality, understands how to get the crowd to stand up and get dancing and is continuously familiar with the ever-changing patterns in the music industry.

Chapter 5: Establishing Games For Occasions

In case you are a DJ at a club or play at occasions, odds are that you are going to wish to separate the crowd a bit, let them mix a bit and likewise establish some game that the crowd can play not just for entertainment yet likewise get them to mix a bit. You have more than likely been to wedding events where dance games are played to captivate the crowd. You ought to have the ability to do this if you are going to achieve success as a DJ.

The old Hokey Pokey is among the staples at all wedding events. You can put your own spin to this prominent game when you serve as a DJ. You can play your own kind of spin for this tune along with others that are typically utilized for game functions. It is excellent to separate the dancing with games for the crowd as it gets individuals to join one another a bit more and makes them have a ball.

You must search for various kinds of dance games that might work when you are practicing as a DJ. This is particularly crucial at wedding events and occasions. Ensure that the games that you establish for clubs or occasions are suitable for the occasions that you are hosting as a DJ. For instance, if you are hired for a celebration for children, the exact same games will probably not be suitable for nightclubs.

You can discover games to establish for your DJ occasions right online. There are a variety of various games that a DJ utilizes to separate the crowd. This is an outstanding method to get the crowd moving as well as a method to wind a crowd down. You can likewise utilize a game as a method to detract individuals from anything that fails throughout the course of the occasion to get individuals back into the swing of things and far from anything that may have distracted them throughout the course of the night.

At the conclusion of the night, or day, depending upon the kind of DJ celebration that you are hosting, you are likewise going to wish to wind individuals down. The majority of the time, you may do this with a game and after that reveal one last song. You must make the tunes towards completion of the celebration or closing of the club. This is when you wish to begin signifying to the visitors that it is time to leave.

By captivating those at the celebration or the club with some dancing games, you can be an enjoyable DJ. You will separate the regimen of simply dancing and enable individuals to have some enjoyment joining one another. If you intend on hosting a wedding event, you ought to ensure that you get guidelines from the family regarding the games that you wish to play. Lots of families will anticipate the regular favorites that are at other wedding events and might be dissatisfied if you ruin the wedding by not playing particular DJ games.

In many cases, a family might want you to supply them with particular ethnic associated DJ games for occasions. There are numerous various games that anybody who wishes to be DJ needs to understand before they begin any occasion. The most essential thing that you need to understand is what individuals want and that you offer them with what they desire in a manner that they will be gratified.

Chapter 6: Getting Your First Gig

Odds are that your initial gig as a DJ will be something little and perhaps even family-related. The very best odds you have of getting a gig is via a relative or by hosting a wedding event or some other celebration. While you wait for your huge opportunity to end up being a DJ at a club, you might need to make ends meet by doing DJ work at a range of various functions. Wedding events are a big deal and you most likely will begin with something tinier than that.

It is essential that you take your DJ duties seriously no matter what kind of gig you get. You are going to get work by word of mouth as a DJ. This holds true even if you work in a club. If you have an excellent credibility, one of appearing on time, making individuals delighted, playing the appropriate music and doing your work, you will get great recommendations. If you have a bad track record, word is going to get around. Regardless of how gifted you believe you are, no matter how excellent of an entertainer you believe you are, you need to offer individuals what they desire otherwise you are not going to obtain any more work. It is as easy as that.

Make certain that you evaluate all of your devices before your initial gig. You must have a respectable concept of what individuals desire when you do this gig in addition to any special demands for tracks. You ought to ask whoever is hiring you for the gig if there are any tracks that they want performed at the occasion or any games. See to it that you have the music and that you do a trial run. The majority of the time, occasions where somebody works with a DJ is a once in a lifetime occasion. For you, this is simply a project, but for some individuals, they prepare this occasion for months and in many cases, even years. In a lot of cases, it is a once in a lifetime occasion.

You ought to discuss your routine with the individual who hires you for the occasion. Make certain that there is absolutely nothing that you are overlooking. If, for some reason, you are doing a wedding event, the visitors, along with those in the wedding event, are going to depend upon you to keep the celebration going and to ensure that you make everybody pleased with the music.

It is an excellent idea to begin your DJ profession playing for wedding events or other occasions. This can not just get you used to performing in front of audiences, yet it can likewise provide you cash that you require to improve your tools and get more music. Just as somebody who is trying to find an acting job will frequently take another job in a field near acting, you ought to likewise take a job that will foot the bill and still allow you to go after your dreams of spinning disks.

You can not anticipate to stroll into a club and take control of on your opening night. You can, nevertheless, continue to go to clubs and search for jobs whilst you are not engaged doing paying gigs. The moment that you get your initial job at a club, you can after that pay more focus to your music mixing than you do at your wedding event DJ ventures. In the meantime, you will have made ample cash to have actually amassed more music along with better tools.

If you are searching for a paying DJ job at a brand-new club, the most effective method to do so is to speak with the owner and after that produce a demonstration tape. You can offer to work one night in the club as a test. You must never ever offer to work for free, nevertheless. Strangely enough, individuals who offer to work for free are not taken as seriously in any type of industry as those who require payment. By creating a demonstration tape and speaking with the club owner, you might have the ability to get a job.

Do not expect your initial DJ gig spinning records to be on a Saturday or Friday night, as well. Odds are that you are going to be offered a job throughout the week. You are going to need to work your way up towards the greater paying gigs as you continue to amaze the crowd and acquire an audience. Club owners have an interest in earning a profit in their club. The more individuals you pull in, the more they consume. The more the people consume, the more cash the club makes. That indicates that if you have a following, you are going to be promoted. This is how it functions when you are working as a DJ in a venue.

Constantly be a professional. Constantly evaluate your tools before you even start. Ensure that you research the club before you even begin so that you understand what kind of music that they play and what individuals like. Bear in mind that scene from "The Blues Brothers?" Where the blues band strolled into a Country music bar to play the blues? It was amusing in that movie, yet will not be amusing in case you do this in a real club. Make certain that you understand what they like and provide the people what they enjoy.

This does not imply that you need to be a duplicate of every other DJ in that club. You slowly wish to begin to bring your own mix and your own character to the club. For your initial gig, you might even wish to play one of your personal mixes. See how the audience responds.

Being a DJ in a club or perhaps a wedding event implies practice. Do not anticipate to set the world ablaze on the opening night. Your objective must be to develop a steady group of fans who arrive to the club and who like what you spin. Eventually, you are going to be asked to get those Saturday night gigs.

Chapter 7 - How To Promote Your Business

Whether you have a wedding event, DJ company or if you are a club DJ, you will wish to promote your company as much as feasible. The most convenient method to accomplish this is to approach friends and family. Make certain that if you are set up to perform in a club that you have as many friends and family present as possible. In this industry of being a DJ, you are going to get the majority of your business by word of mouth. So you ought to make sure that as many individuals know about your business as conceivable.

One manner in which you can advertise your business is to offer your services free of charge at an occasion for friends and family. This must be an occasion that is not only for friends and family, yet will likewise consist of other visitors. You ought to have cards that you give out to others so that they can hire you for the gig. In case you do an excellent job at your initial job, odds are that you will get others.

Another method to advertise your business is to join your regional Chamber of Commerce. Many individuals who are brand-new in the area and trying to find the services that you offer are going to look to the chamber to help them choose which are the most reliable businesses in the area. By signing up with such a group, you are adding trustworthiness to your business.

Constantly have your business cards handy. You never ever know who you are going to encounter. In case you are working as a wedding event DJ and additionally have ambitions to spin disks, you ought to have two cards printed. Ensure that you offer the suitable card to the appropriate individual. Strike up discussions with those at celebrations and other occasions where you meet individuals. Once again, this is a business where individuals usually get the person from 'somebody they know."

In case you have a gig, you must inform those who have an interest in your services to come by. They can have a look at how you perform to determine if they wish to employ you. By constantly being at your finest, you stand a much greater chance of acquiring more business.

Constantly appear on time. Constantly ensure that your tools work. Have a "plan B" in the event of anything malfunctioning. While there are some things that you can not do anything about, there are methods to back up your devices. A generator, for instance, can assist if you have a power failure. Be versatile when it concerns performing. This is necessary when you are handling individuals. Often individuals will state that they desire something when they actually desire another. Do not get irritated, however ensure that you have the ability to alter your strategies. Nothing needs to be engraved in stone, even though you do wish to have a performance strategy in mind when you are working as a DJ.

Having cards printed is inexpensive and may be done online. You must additionally promote your company if you are operating at a club by having leaflets printed to promote yourself at the club. You can hand these out and even put the leaflets in neighborhood shops. You can get more individuals to come to the club by doing this.

Charity events are another method to advertise your operation. You can contribute your time to a charity event, meet an entire brand-new group of individuals who will not just enjoy your music, however will additionally appreciate you for offering yourself to a charity cause. You can frequently get company by doing this and numerous bands, along with those who serve as DJ s, will offer their time to such occasions.

You must constantly be promoting your operation. Make an excuse to speak about your company to those who you meet. You never ever know if the person you meet in the elevator has a buddy who is opening up a brand-new bar and is searching for a DJ.

Chapter 8: Guidelines For DJ Professionals

When you work as a DJ professional, you are a self-employed individual. This suggests that you pay your own taxes and that you are going to need to state any earnings that you make. It likewise suggests that you can deduct your tools along with other costs for your company. The most intelligent thing that you can do when you end up being a DJ is to incorporate your company. This releases you from any individual liability in the event somebody chooses to take legal action versus you for any reason at all.

A corporation is a different entity. It can have a tax number, it can open a checking account, it could be sued. Keep your individual assets separate from your corporation to secure them in the event of any legal lawsuits. The majority of the time, a DJ does not need to fret about getting sued. However in the litigious world in which we live, it is most ideal to secure yourself. You are going to additionally get a tax break if you choose to incorporate your company rather than running as a sole proprietor. You can remove gas mileage and also a van for you to bring your devices around when you do your taxes. You need to have a tax accounting professional prepare your taxes. In case you intend on entering into business on your own, do it right.

You need to additionally have insurance coverage. You can get event insurance coverage quickly through your regional insurance provider. For instance, if something falls on somebody, you can be guaranteed versus liability. You ought to constantly be ready for anything when you work for yourself as a professional.

Get your cash upfront, or at minimum get a deposit before you reserve any engagement. This is the primary guideline for anybody who is serving as a DJ, specifically for a celebration or a wedding event. You must have all of your cash upfront before you even begin to perform. You ought to request a deposit to hold the date and after that request for your cash before you begin to perform. Among the groups of individuals who get cheated the most frequently, sadly, are entertainers. The wedding event is over, the bride and groom have actually departed and the parent of the bride is mad that you didn't play a tune that he desired that he didn't even inform you to play. And he's had a couple of drinks. How do you get your cash? Taking him to court costs you time along with cash. You are much better off to prevent this from taking place by getting paid in advance. Lots of entertainers request a cashier's check or money before they are going to perform to stop this from taking place.

Have a contract available for anybody to sign in case they engage you to perform. This is additionally required. In case of any legal lawsuits, you will not win in case you do not have anything in writing. Define all of your responsibilities ahead of time and after that have the individual who is hiring you sign the agreement. You sign a copy too so that each of you have a copy of the agreement. It ought to define the cost, the terms of payment and the tasks that are to be carried out. Ensure that you satisfy the commitments under the agreement.

These are guidelines for anybody who wishes to begin their own company. Many individuals who start as a DJ wish to make some money on the side and will not take actions to secure themselves. You are much better off to commence your DJ company as a genuine business from the start. Not only will you be securing yourself, yet you will likewise seem more professional in the eyes of other folks.

In case you operate in a club, you will more than likely be hired under contract or, in states that are hire at will, you will not have a contract yet work from week to week. You ought to constantly require a contract for a particular time period. Tinier clubs might not provide this, yet the bigger clubs are going to typically provide contracts for their entertainers. A hire at will state is a state in which somebody could be fired at will, without notification, and for any reason. Learn if you reside in a hire at will state before you start performing.

If you are not sure about an agreement that you are signing, take it to a lawyer who will have the ability to clarify it for you. A contract is a lawfully binding commitment. If you sign an agreement with a club owner, odds are that the agreement is going to be prepared in favor of the club owner. The more of a following you have with the club, the more leverage you have when it concerns generating income.

You must likewise ensure that you are getting paid by the club regularly. If you see that company is falling and you are not earning money, it might be time to try to find a fresh club. One of the regrettable aspects of operating in this sector is that brand-new clubs open and close all of the time. Typically, those who are ripped off are those who are owed cash, like the contractors. So make sure that you get compensated when you are supposed to be compensated.

Safeguard your interests whenever you are a DJ or if you remain in any other kind of business. You might enjoy music. You might enjoy performing for other individuals. You might like the club environment and the love of the club. However if at the end of the night you are not making money, you need to search for your cash or discover another club. An agreement is the very best manner in which you can safeguard yourself from getting stiffed whenever you are performing as a DJ. Regrettably, if the club declares bankruptcy, you will probably not see your cash. That is why you must ensure you are paid regularly when you work for a club owner.

Chapter 9: How To Acquire A Club Job

A club job is the dream job of anybody who wishes to spin disks and end up being a DJ. However it takes some time to land the dream job. You are going to need to operate at a great deal of other clubs, tinier clubs, before you land the huge job. You need to take the suggestions provided in the previous chapter when it concerns working for these tinier clubs along with the bigger clubs.

When you have a following, you can then look for a job at a big club where you can generate income or, in many cases, a portion of the earnings of the club. The option is yours. Much of those who operate in this sector choose to take a percentage instead of a flat fee. In many cases, the DJ ends up being part-owner of the club. When individuals begin to go to a club due to the fact that they like the person who is spinning the disks and mixing the music, club owners see that and will frequently provide a piece of the club as a method to compensate the DJ.

A DJ does not need to stop there. There are some who go on to perform as artists in their own right. If you have singing skill, for instance, you might want to search for more popularity in the recording industry. As soon as you have actually made a name for yourself as a talented entertainer, you might discover that other doors open for you in the show business.

To get a job at a trendy club, you are going to require more than simply a demonstration tape and a couple of fans. You are going to need to have a resume of clubs where you have actually worked. You must constantly continue to look to improve yourself when it concerns playing as a DJ in clubs so that you might succeed. As it was pointed out previously, clubs reoccur. Music changes. Patterns change. So it is necessary that you strike while the iron is hot and continue to produce greater objectives for yourself so that you can continue to rise.

You need to make as many connections with club owners as conceivable in order to get an opportunity to perform in their clubs. The greatest clubs are those that lie in the bigger cities, so it might be required for you to transfer if this is the job that you wish to have. New York City and Los Angeles are the prime locations where the sought-after clubs are. In case you get in with one of the sought-after clubs, you can make a great deal of cash and enjoy your prosperous profession as a disk spinning DJ.

Concluding chapter: Getting A Mechanic Permit To Play Music

Wait a minute, you are going to perform other individuals's music in order to earn a profit? There is something that you need to understand before you end up being a sought-after DJ. You need to have a permit for this. A mechanical permit or mechanic permit allows you to perform a track for profit that is under license by another person. These are easy to get. Nor do you need to haggle with the individual who owns the catalog in the majority of locations.

The Harry Fox Agency is the location where you wish to go to get a permit to perform a track for profit. Due to the fact that the tunes that you are utilizing are probably under copyright, you do not wish to run the risk of copyright violation by performing these tunes without a permit. The Harry Fox agency manages the majority of the licensing for all tunes that are under copyright and you can obtain a license for utilizing the tunes for a small fee. If you are performing music at your sibling's wedding event, odds are that you can get away with it without having a permit. However in case you get to the point where you are popular and are making significant money as DJ, then you need to have a permit to utilize the music to earn a profit.

While you are at it, if you create a mix that individuals like, you must copyright it on your own. You can do this quickly by sending your music to the copyright office. It costs a fee to do this, however nobody else is going to have the ability to utilize your music for profit unless they compensate you. That suggests that even if the track is played on the radio, they need to pay you royalties.

In case you have any concerns about copyright law or how to get a permit for tracks that you wish to utilize for profit, you must speak to a lawyer who deals with copyright law. Once again, you might not need to do this when you are initially beginning - it is not likely that anybody will come after you for copyright violation if you are simply working a little club or playing at wedding events. However as you end up being larger in the market, you will wish to make certain that you comprehend how copyright works to safeguard your own work in addition to making certain that you safeguard yourself from claims of copyright violation. For the most part, the worst thing that will take place is that you are going to get a Cease and Desist order if you are utilizing a specific track. Nevertheless, the larger you get and the more cash you make, the more you stand to lose if you are encroaching on copyrighted product.

You can end up being a DJ if you have an understanding of music, a passion of music and a wish to perform. You can get going with only a little bit of tools and begin to acquire paying gigs immediately, probably right in your own town. You can try out music so that you get the sound that you like. If you have a natural appreciation for music and enjoy mixing audio, this might be the perfect career option for you.

I hope that you have enjoyed this book and that you have found it useful. If you want to share your thoughts on this book, you can do so by leaving a review on the Amazon page. Have a great rest of the day.

Printed in Great Britain
by Amazon

71970054R00031